THE ROXY MIX

Poems

Bud R. Berkich

Cyberwit.net
HIG 45 Kaushambi Kunj, Kalindipuram
Allahabad - 211011 (U.P.) India
http://www.cyberwit.net
Tel: +(91) 9415091004
E-mail: info@cyberwit.net

Printed at Repro India Limited.

For Roxy, for someday...

When You Are Old

When you are old and grey and full of sleep,
And nodding by the fire, take down this book,
And slowly read, and dream of the soft look
Your eyes had once, and of their shadows deep;

How many loved your moments of glad grace,
And loved your beauty with love false or true,
But one man loved the pilgrim soul in you,
And loved the sorrows of your changing face;

And bending down beside the glowing bars,
Murmur, a little sadly, how Love fled
And paced upon the mountains overhead
And hid his face amid a crowd of stars.

—William Butler Yeats

THE ROXY MIX

Acknowledgments

Special thanks to my parents: Evelyn Jean Rohs (1936-1980), Rose Ellen Berkich (1910-1993) and Peter Lee Berkich (1923-1981). To my writing mentor and friend James Stephen Merrill ("Steve") (1943-2006) for reading the very first draft and providing helpful and honest criticism. Thanks also to the Borders Poetry Group (Bridgewater, NJ) and the following members for also listening to readings of the manuscript and providing useful commentary: Sandra Barlow, Anthony Frangione, Robert Rosenbloom, Paul Sohar and Ellen Zinn. And finally, thanks to Dr. Agrawal at Cyberwit.net for (finally!) making this project a reality.

Contents

I. BEGINNINGS

(c. 12/29/04-1/25/05)

"Shall I compare thee to a summer's day?
Thou art more lovely and more temperate:
Rough winds do shake the darling buds of May,
And summer's lease hath all too short a date..."

(From "Sonnet 18"— William Shakespeare)

Flirt

You come
out from back,
decked out
in black

knee-high,
platform boots;
frilly, short skirt;
clingy, tight top—

direct eye
contact—

STOP!

"How are ya doin'?"
"I'm fine, and you?" (A
I-know-you're-checking-
me-out-and-I-like-it

grin—)
lingering
past the bookshelf.

Seeing is Believing

At this point,
I'm not quite sure
what you think of me
(although the prospects look good),

but I'm pretty sure
you sense that
I like you
(you're right, I do); so—

let's
take it slow
and easy,
and from there—

we'll see,
we'll see.

Special Order

A Godsend
is what I call you
and all you are you

have given
freely,
selflessly,
innocently—

and what you mean
to me

         is the free-

dom

to be
me.

Atom Heart Mother and You— Meditations

First things first.

Says who?
Anyway,

I would like to
preface this
by saying—

Atom Heart Mothers?
I've known a few.

But definitely not *you*,
my cute little
heavy metal girl—

girl of my dreams,
the girl that wants
to marry Eddie Vedder—

over my dead body, Eddie.

Wait!

Without further hesitation,
let's begin our meditation:

I.

"Mind your throats, please,
and try not to get your milky
all over my funky dung."

"I'm the father around here,
and I'll shout if I want to.
I'm like a bad dream—
I keep on coming back,
remerging."

By
the by—

John Aldiss rocks.
Heeeeerrrrre's Johnny!

II.

If   I had you—
I would be happy.
No ifs about it.

III.

How do you feel—
about me?
State exactly.

Don't worry—
I like you
and I care.

How do you feel?
Just you let me know.
Just you.

IV.

Lying with you
under a fat old sun
as it's falling,
church bells calling
and the cut grass
smelling so sweet,

hand in hand—

sing to me,
sing to me.

Visions of Gilmour
on top of a reservoir
with a Fender Stratocaster
(nowhere to plug in the amp)
belting out
his Fat Old Sun solo
with me down here below,

fishing for trophies
at midnight.

V.

With the sink faucet
dripping *ad infinitum*—

Alan's breakfast is officially over,
psychedelically speaking, of course.

(Please take note that this Compact Disc
was touched   by her   my favorite register girl.)

So give it a big hug and kiss
for the love of Jesus. And, hey—

can I get a witness?

Selfish

Some had it
and then lost it.

But not me. In fact,
I never had it
in the first place.

So, I have nothing to lose. No,
I have *everything* to lose. Yes,

you are everything to me,
and if I lose you,
I lose everything,
guaranteed.

So, with what little
I *don't* have,
I'm going to give it
all I've got. After all,

they don't know what they're missing.
But who cares?
All I have or don't have is yours (not theirs),
and I don't want you to miss it—

any of it. That's all I care about.

One Thing Not

If I was in Paradise
I'd find something wrong, but

I must
say—

so
far,
so
good

in
every
way—

but in
this,
not.

To you,
I am
unnameable—

like a
Beckett
novel.

I have
been
reduced

to a pronoun.

Why?

Is it
me?
Is it

you?
Is it
he?
Is it
they?

What?

Please—
identify.

1/21

After your
success

in making
me late

to leave
by fifteen minutes,

you found it
rather amusing.

(So did I.)

"Now see what I
made you do?

"What would you
do without Roxy?"

(Good question.)

"I don't know,"
I replied,

"but that's
why I'm here."

And that's the truth—
nothing but.

Out of the Vortex

You said it.
You know it.

(Now I know
you do.) So,

my dear, please
forgive me my
ignorance in ever
doubting you.

(If not you,
who?)

The Vortex
again?

No way.

I don't want to be
sucked back into
that darkness.

As Millay
would say—

"All right,
Go ahead!
What's in a name?"

My dear,
lock me in
or lock me out,
I don't care.

Just so you
have the key,
and you're there.

Shine

I'm walking in the light,
because you flicked
the switch
on all my darkness.

(Another turned the lights out.)

Now, to me,
you are an angel
of light—

bright and
beautiful—

on the
inside
and out.

So shine—

you great
girl, you.

No Return

I often find myself
having conversations
with you, even when
you're not there.

Nothing new—
I used to do it
with *her*, too—

only difference is
that she wasn't there
when, in fact, she was.

Not a minute
of a day
goes by
without you in it—

like today
when I found myself
saying to myself—

"Five hours until
Roxy's here,
four hours until
Roxy's here,
three
two
one—

it's Roxy time." And then,
"How do I get close to her?
What do I say?
What will she say to me?
How will I respond?"

Etc.,
etc.,

etc.—
ad infinitum.

Maybe it's crazy.
Maybe *I'm* crazy.
(Or getting there.)
Maybe I'm cracking up.

But if this is insanity,
then custom fit that
straight jacket,

a few more electric shocks,
please!

(so I can bounce off
these padded walls
with authority)

and make sure that
lobotomy is a
nice, clean break
with any reality
other than you.

Girl— you're a crazy little trip
with a one-way ticket—

and I'm not coming back.

1/25

After the events
of 1/21,

I decided that
it was time

to throw the proverbial
pass into the end zone.

And I did.

At this point,
the ball is still
in the air,

and you *have*
to come down
with it, my dear—

even if you are
double-covered.

II. ILLUSIONS

(1/26/05-2/18/05)

"'Faith' is a fine invention
When Gentlemen can *see*—
But *Microscopes* are prudent
In an Emergency."

("185"— Emily Dickinson)

Holding Pattern

What is holding
you back, my dear?

Is it him? (Ha!)

Let it be known
that I have nothing
but faith in you.

Feel privileged—
there's not many
I do—

but you—
yes, you!
I definitely
do you.

For what
are you waiting?
Hesitating?

(By now, I should be celebrating, but)

my dear, for you—
I'll wait.

Just so there's no confusion...

this is not sex.
This is not sex.
This is not sex.

This is love.
This is love.
This is love.

Letter

Something concrete,
something obvious
would be nice—

instead of all this
cloak and dagger stuff.

I feel like I'm
in the dark—

a joke, and everyone
else knows the punch line.

OK, I give, already.
A little help— please?

Addressed to:

God,
Roxy,
members of "The Conspiracy,"

all of the above.

Signed,

Confused and frustrated

PS: Have some mercy on a novice—
        I'm new at this!

Touchdown?

A conspiracy—

    to bring us together,

or to keep us apart?

    A ride home—

the deciding factor

    (I hope).

Super Bowl Sunday?

    Damn straight.

But more like

    Super Bowl Monday.

Looks like that pass

    is finally gonna come down.

Newton's Law

It's still up in the air.

And that's good.
For as long as it is,
the following phrase still applies:

"What goes up
must come back down."

Eventually. And when it does—
more than an end
zone
will be found,
a beginning— together.

Coming Down

And it's— intercepted!
in the end zone. (Or,
at least, batted away.)

So, place the ball out
at the twenty or the thirty—
whatever—

It's OK. I think I
understand. There's
absolutely nothing wrong.

We'll just line up
on the line of scrimmage,
get back in the trenches
and dig in, so to speak.

After all, it's still early
in the first quarter.
Let's just get the ball back
and do it again. Start out
first and ten, if you will.

All of this football imagery—
it would drive you mad.

I promise I'll stop.

Saint Valentine's Day, 2005

So it is.
And once again,
insignificant—
alone.

My mind hearkens
back to high school
and French Club,
when they would sell
Carnations for good
intentions. Yes—
the road to Hell
is paved with
good intentions
(and most likely
strewn with the
Carnations of
past loves.) The
Carnations that I
never got. Not a
red one (definitely
not), not even a
yellow—

    poor fellow,
you. (Self-pity stinks,
but *God*—

I hate this day.) Anyway,

you're with him,
he's with you,
and the only way
I'm with you
on this day
(which was more
than likely
instituted by

Sade, not Valentine)
is in my heart.

And what about you?
Where do I hold
a place in you?

Is it in your heart,
or only in your head?
(Or mine.) Is it
first place,
or second,
or third?
Do I even show up?
(I hope so.)
I would hate to be
an also-ran.

You go through the motions
of going through the motions
on this day (*his* day, not mine),
but as in the institution of marriage
(a shaky proposition at best),
what will tomorrow find?

Possibly— him out,
and you with me. But,
as I said to you
in another poem—

we'll see,
we'll see.

And no doubt
we will,

in time.

Not There, Here

I wish that I
could do or say
something to show
you how much I care,

more than I'm doing
(can do) now, but
as far as I know,
I can't.

I wish that I could
give you back the
feeling that you
seemed to feel
when we first met,

one of intimacy—
the touch of a hand,
the feel of your
scarf on my back,
words said in relative
secret, but said
just the same. And
the look in your eyes
that couldn't disguise
the depth below the surface.

Where has it gone? Or is it
still there, only a different

manifestation? Another dispensation
that takes a while getting used to?

I can't help feeling
responsible for the difference
I sense you sense now—
maybe I should have never
gone beyond the now we had
at that particular present, but

I hope you would understand
somehow. Or maybe there's
a positive in all of this
seeming negative (do I imagine it?)

Or is it actual? Tangible? There?

It seems that you are quiet these days,
which is better than silent, I guess,
but maybe your quietness
speaks volumes, more or less.

Am I deaf
to your silence?

Or am I merely
hearing without listening?

If so, be my hearing aid.
Tune me in to your megahertz.
Vibrate me to the subtle rhythms
of your unique hemisphere—

in a world undiscovered
not there (with him), but
with me—

      still waiting—

            for you (after him)—

              here—

in my world,
my monomaniacal hell,

Here.

INTERMISSION

(2/18/05- 2/28/05)

"I loafe and invite my soul,
I lean and loafe at my ease observing a spear of summer grass."

(From "Song of Myself"— Walt Whitman)

At the break...

a void. Without

you— alone. I

got the Roxy blues.

Hell is anyplace without God.
No. Hell is anyplace without Roxy.

Heart? Yes.
Head? Yes.
Here? No. Not.

Not yet, anyway. But
back up a second.

What were you getting at
the other night?

"Do you live with friends?" (No.)

Out of context? Or in the
context of

"Are you going anywhere?" (No.)

Home? Yes.
Alone? Yes. Yes,

home alone. (Like the Macaulay kid.) But

what I want to know is,

are you going to do something about it?
(Me alone, not Macaulay.) Please do.

After all,

I don't want to star
in my own pathetic comedy.

Meditation 21

I don't look at
an event in isolation.

I look at an event
as a continuum.

In relation to
a series of other events,

the event being
a part of the whole—

a synecdoche,
if you will.

No event is
an island.

Rather, a part
of the whole. And

concerning the events
that concern you and me,

there's a string
of them stretching

from the moment
of our beginnings

until the now
of our present.

Some would say
a whole lot of nothing,

but I would say
that nothing is something—

for the densest molecule
is basically quantum space.

And to think of you and me
in terms of a continuum

and not merely
in isolation

is for *this*
armchair scientist

not that much
of a quantum leap.

Wondering Aloud

No, this isn't a Jethro Tull song.
I was just sitting here thinking.
And I know I said that I
wouldn't do it again but, please—
indulge me just this once—
if I'm totally off-base about this,
please forgive me.

What if that pass in the end zone
never came down? What if
it was never intercepted? What if
it's still up in the air?

Concert? What concert?
S— didn't know the name
of the band— pre-*post facto* and
more surprisingly, ex-*post facto*.
I have a hunch you didn't, either.
Because there wasn't a band
or a concert to go to in the first place.

What if it all was part of the plan?
What if it all was part of the Conspiracy
to gauge a reaction? If so, then when
are they gonna go into action
on our behalf? (Do you even know
what the hell I'm talking about?) Do I?

Listen. If I had asked someone
to go with me somewhere
to get away from someone else
and the primary someone wouldn't dare,
I for one am not going
to end up going with that someone else
that I'm trying to get away from.
(Are you getting all of this?)

Conspiracy? Yes. I believe so.

There's just too much to say no.
But what I *don't* know
is how much of this do you know?
All of it? A part of it? Or,
are you totally in the dark about it—
like me?

Anyway, I just want to say thanks—
for everything. And either way,
I still love you no less.

Here's to the day
where there is no Conspiracy,
real or imagined;
when there is no someone,
primary or secondary.

Here's to the day
when there's only you and me—
real, not imagined—

a great day, indeed.

The Eyes Have It

I must admit
that I feel
rather vulnerable
this week
away from you.

You know,
like being on
an airplane,
and your life
is basically
in someone else's hands?

If that sucker
should malfunction
well, there's really
not a hell of a lot
you can do about it,
now is there?

So, I guess
you could say
that I feel
a little
out of control
(not that I
would ever want
to control you,
my dear).

But it's at times
like these that I
remember the look
in your eyes
when we first met—
a look that went
beyond mere recognition—
and what it said to me.

And this—
more than anything else—
can hold me together
until I have the privilege
of seeing those
pretty eyes again.

III. FRUSTRATIONS

(3/1/05-3/18/05)

"Do not go gentle into that good night.
Rage, rage against the dying of the light."

(From "Do Not Go Gentle into That Good Night"— Dylan
Thomas)

God's Girl

I'm starting to call you
"God's girl." Do you like it?
It fits you perfectly.

In other words,
the girl that God chose
above all the others
to get me over the other.

And you have accomplished
your task flawlessly.
Maybe a little too well—
for now I see no other,
other than you.

And I wouldn't have it
any other way. Except

for the fact that
I hardly ever see you.

So I pray: "God, when
is she going to stop
being *your* girl, and
start being *mine*?"

As Marvell writes:
"Had we but world enough, and time;
This coyness, lady, were no crime."

Exactly, Andy. And
as it stands now, my dear,
we're talking
major felony, here.

Stagnant.

Nothing moving.

Nada.

Zilch.

No forward progress.

Nothing.

Not.

No.

This is the present.

Our present.

At present.

In the present.

Now.

Now what?

Divine Comedy

Just as Borges
had his Beatrices,
you are my Beatrice.

But you are still off
with your pseudo-Dante,
while I'm still mired here
deep within the ninth circle

of Hell. In search of
a Virgil to lead me out,

but you know and I know
that the only way I'm
getting to Paradise
is through you—
my salvation.

You saved me once.
Now it remains
to be seen if you
can do it again.

At least try—
for even Dante
got a smile
(and Borges
got the girl)
in the end.

Voided:

a puzzle
missing

a single piece. Worthless:

garbage man fodder,
fireplace fuel.

Voided II

I stand before you now

voided. A puzzle

missing a single piece.

Worthless—

fodder for the garbage man,

fuel for the fireplace.

Good Faith Estimate

Like a loan officer

with a thirty-year fixed,

I'm "floating" your

interest rate, so to speak,

to "lock you in"

at the most strategic time.

So, don't go and take your loan

to another mortgage company. And

don't worry. I won't go and sell it

to someone else.

Experiment

Have you ever read
later Beckett
in his claustrophobic stage?

When the protagonists,
usually just one woman
or a man and a woman,

are put inside a very small
enclosure; barely breathing,
naked, their bodies contorted
in various uncomfortable,
compromising positions—

exposed to alternating extremes
of intense light and darkness,
varying degrees of hot and cold—

with no way out, or at least
the determination and/or the strength
to find one?

And the worst part of it all
is that at no time whatsoever
does the victim(s) (or the reader,
for that matter) get a clue
as to who has put them
in this state in the first place.

That's how I feel we are now.

Someone unseen
is working behind the scenes
to keep us apart,
claustrophobe us,
keep us as lab rats
in their pathetic
little Skinner Box,

to observe how we respond
to their sadistic stimuli.

Well, no more.
For I promise you
that I will find out
who this little God
wannabe is, and I
will turn she, he,
they or it over
to the One
to be dealt with
inside His eternal labyrinth—
toys for the Minotaur to play with.

In truth,
the answer
is in the cards.

Reversal

Dr. Shuller said
"don't give in to forces,"
and he was right.

They are slowly squeezing
us to a bloody pulp,
like two lemons.

Let them.

We'll take the juice,
made lemonade,
open up a lemonade stand

and sell it to
the bastards
with interest.

Intimate Strangers

If my unseen
counterpart and I
should somehow
trade places
with each other,

then he would know
what it is
not to have you,
to be in need of you,

and I would know
what it is
to have you always,
to never want again.

This knowledge would
most likely mean that
we would be able to
understand and sympathize
with each other totally,

which would eventually
result in us becoming
the best of friends.

That's why, for your sake,
I prefer to remain anonymous.

Variations I

The change to effect a change?
Maybe.

An open window of opportunity?
Maybe.

A chance to lose myself in your bliss?
Maybe.

An opportunity I wouldn't miss?
Definitely.

Variations II

If the window
is open,

climb through.

I'll be
waiting

for you—

on the
other

side.

Variations III

If by this change
there's a chance
the window
should open,
climb through—

I'll be there
waiting

for you—

in a
peaceful field,
on the

      other side.

Adapt

Seeing you even less
than the little I have
will still not lessen
my love for you

in the least. In fact,
this could be a blessing
in disguise.

For maybe,
just maybe,
this change
will change
the existing
status quo
that binds
you to him
24/7.

If something
such as that
should come
of this,

then I'll
gladly
settle
for less,

to lose
myself
in your
bliss.

Girl—
I wouldn't
miss

that for
the world.

3/18

What are they trying to do
to you, my girl,
what are they trying to do?
You, who are the sweetest girl
God ever put on His blue and green Earth,
who would never hurt anyone—
what are they trying to do?
Just who the hell do they think they are?

They don't know you,
are not close to you,
don't know what it means
to walk in your light,
to feel your power
like I do—

they have the audacity to judge you,
who are better than ten of them—
they could learn a thing or two from you.

As I told you, my dear,
you look nice. You always look nice.
You have absolutely nothing
of which to be ashamed.
Don't give in to them and their petty jealousy.
Jealous because they can't wear what you wear
(they could, but who would care?).
But my caring goes beyond mere surface tendencies
to the you of you. I love you to death. I do.

And I will always be there for you,
no matter what.

Why? Because you
were there for me. When?
When you pulled me
out of The Vortex
with nothing more or less than you. And you alone.

For that, I will defend you
until there's no more fortress to defend.
But even if there were no Vortex,
I would still be enchanted
by your charm, a light more brighter
than the blackest of black holes.

We have to take this to another level, my dear—
learn to color outside the Borders, so to speak.
With the walls of this Beckett cylinder
closing in, we must transcend.

Would you do that?
At some point, please.
I know now that three months of building
have not been in vain. The foundation
stands; stalwart, immutable.

I know this because
when I stood before you
that night— in a lot of ways
the night of nights— one
thought entered my mind

and spoke to me lines
of epic proportion:

she confided in you.
She confided in you.
She confided, in *you*.

IV. DEPARTURES

(3/19/05- 4/1/05)

"...when I try to imagine a faultless love
Or the life to come, what I hear is the murmur
Of underground streams, what I see is a limestone landscape."

(From "In Praise of Limestone"— W.H. Auden)

Cupid

I don't want this to be
merely an artistic endeavor.
Like it was with her—
thirty-one poems,
a play to figure her out,
and a short story
(the genesis of the play,
by the way) that resulted in a
prose piece, all to figure her out.

But girl, I don't need to figure *you* out.
You're the real deal—
what you see is what you get—
and that's quite a lot. But
I want more. I want
the total package— all of you.
We're not talking some fantasy here,
this is not lust, no. Far from it.
This is love that goes beyond
mere friendship. You mean a lot to me—
so much so that I hesitate to use
the word "friend," so as not to belittle it.

Now, don't get me wrong— I am your friend,
always was, always will be— and I
consider you mine, one of my closest,
even though I've never been as close
to you as I would like to be, as I know

that we could be, if given the chance,
the opportunity.

And unlike her (you're so unlike her—
to your advantage—) I believe that God
has a plan for us yet— more than art—
which is there— thirty-six poems plus
this, and more to come. And oh,
by the way, you now lead the league
in poetry— none of my former Beatrices

have even an eighth of what you have
(and the one that comes closest I sometimes
feel shouldn't have any, but—) anyway—

consider yourself special,
consider yourself loved.

I digress. But God doesn't.
He sticks to His guns. He's a straight
shooter, and His aim is true. I honestly
believe that there are two arrows
in His bow with our names on them,
pointed straight at me and you.

in medias res I

I'm a satellite
that revolves around my planet—
you. You occupy my center.
You are the middle of it.

Without the pull
of your gravitational field
I will go off my orbit,
hurtling into space.
Alone. Forever.

The farther from the face
of planet you—
the more distant my hell,
the absence of Paradise
away from your presence.

in medias res II

With her,
an artistic endeavor;
thirty-one poems,
a prose piece,
a play—
all to figure her out.

But with you,
what's to figure?
You are the real deal—
what I see
is what I get,
and I get you—
all of you.

So, what is it?
It's like this:
I'm your satellite,
you're my planet.
You are my center,
my world, my existence.

You, my dear,
are the middle of it.

Calling out

to Divine Providence
for something more—

take this to the next level,
hurdle these obstacles—

and get our feet in the door. For

outside the Borderlines
we'll enjoy immunity,

a wealth of opportunity
awaits

you and me.

Alchemy

I feel this night before
like the night before
a big game, or before
a concert on a worldwide tour—
you've been here before,
you've done this before,
but the edge is still there,
and with the edge, the advantage.

What will tomorrow bring?
This resurrection Sunday,
as some would call it—
can we call it that?
Will we be risen to new life?
Will we go on forever in each other,
starting today (it's now 2:30 AM)?

In a way, yes,
for every time I see you
is like new life to me. Like
a resurrection of my body
united with my spirit once again—
breathed back into life by you—
every time that I see you is
like seeing you for the first time.

And the time is *now*. *This* is the time
to act. The time is prime for us to
raise up a relationship that transcends

the death knell of schedules
and situations and obligations which,
in effect, civilize us to no end.

At this time to be Christian,
girl— let's get a little pagan; let's escape
to a place beyond the walls of this
mausoleum and practice some alchemy—
go outside the confines of the city,

(like they did in Zamaytin's *We*,
and the illumination that awaited them there)—
be our own philosopher's stone,
turn some lead into gold
and call it you and me.

Easter Lament, 2005

I'm going in there today,
and I don't care
who sees me;
I don't care what they think,
I don't care what they say,
I—

The best laid plans,
transformed into a
breeding ground of
travesty for
mice and men.

The worst case scenario.
All right, the second-
to-worst case scenario. God
was looking out for me
today, wasn't He? What if
I came fifteen minutes earlier?
Wouldn't *that* have been
the supreme catastrophe?

And pardon my straightforwardness,
but I think that you could do
a whole lot better. No. I *know*
you could. You deserve more.

Three times now I've tried
to go for the pin, and I get

the proverbial kick-out. When
is it going to be my time,
my chance, my opportunity?

What did it mean to you
to see me today— a skater
that falls on his butt, gets up,
and finishes the routine anyway—
even though he knows that points

have been deducted— no win today.

What did it mean? How will you react?
Will you? I was there for *you*. Just you.
But I think you already know that, even though
I took the liberty of telling you anyway.

Even so, I felt like I was invited.
Was there to be something more
today; is that the way you had planned it,
not knowing that he had other plans?

A tap on the knee
with a small hammer
gets a reflex action
almost every time.
Are you that predictable?

Today, I gave you a tap on the knee.
So kick me.

Respond to stimuli.
Try.

Random Thoughts I

Girl— don't think for one instant
that this situation doesn't worry me.
Worried? I'm shitting bricks.
I'm scared. *Damn* scared.

Random Thoughts II

On my way out the door,
the one thing on my mind
that I would have vocalized
if I could was:
"well, I'm leaving you now."

And thinking,
how the same could be
as easily applied to you:

you're leaving me.

Random Thoughts III

Every time I see
you with him,

I get the feeling that
on some level—
either literal
or figurative—

that you are being led;
not leading, not even
wanting to— maybe
not even wanting
to follow. Maybe not even
wanting to be there.

More literal than figurative.

Random Thoughts IV

If you were to leave,
would we go on?
I wonder. Yes—
the foundation is strong,
but what is it supporting?
Anything?

What have I done thus far,
what stud or lolly column
would be the one (the deed)
to carry the weight?

After all,
if you find it difficult now
to make a connection
outside the Borderline,
what would then be like?

I would rather not think about it.

Girl— do me a big favor
and stay right where you are.

We have a lot more building to do.

Confined

to time

within
a box

of concrete

by them,
by him,

and by the
ghost

of her.

I feel
that time

is now
not

on our
side

anymore.

Revolution I

Girl—

don't be
content

to stay
within
the Borders—

get *avant
garde*

get cutting
edge

go outside
the box—

start a
new

artistic
movement

with me—

outside
the perimeter

of this
concrete
shell.

Together,
we'll rule
the art galleries,

we'll determine
the times

for opening
and closing.

Revolution II

The anti
to their
pro

so

reverse
the curse

put her
in her
place

and him
on the shelf

until
confinement

between

the paths
of these

bookcases

is broken
by you

they have
the run
of this
commercial
library

they determine
the books

and who
reads them

V. ENDEAVORS

(4/2/05 - c. 4/25/05)

"April is the cruelest month, breeding
Lilacs out of the dead land, mixing
Memory and desire..."

(From "The Waste Land"— T.S. Eliot)

Pretentious Poem I

Your leaving—
shrouded in mystery—
like her,
more unknown
than known.
But you
are more knowable
than she

and I would like
the opportunity
to be able
to know you
better

but this stymies me.

At this point,
I can't say for certain
that you have
even left

if, in fact,
you have left
the area
of this
concrete box,

I can accept that.
That, actually,

might work to our
advantage. But
what I could
not accept
is if you've
left me,
permanently.

Yes— a decision
must be made
concerning you,
but I need
more information.

Two things
I need now from you:

to know that
you are all right,
and that you will
keep in touch;
that we will continue

in some sense,
in some way—
anyway you see fit,
anyway you can
is good enough for me.

OK.
I'll admit it.
It's a lie.

But I speak truthfully.

Pretentious Poem II

I don't want this poem
or any of these poems
to be your swan song—
to take the place of you.

I said that I
didn't want you
to become
merely
an artistic endeavor
like her
and I meant it.

We made a connection.
But any connection
between two human beings
that is not permanent
is not a connection.
It's an open circuit
through which no energy can flow.

And only you can close the circuit.
Only you can cause the power to come back on.
The Black-Out of '77
couldn't have been as black as this.
This is what it means to be in the dark.
Totally. For there's nothing blacker
than a heart in darkness.

And I don't know what you're going through.
I don't know what happened later that weekend.
All I know is your absence—
here. Now. In this moment. In this instant.

This is my worst fears realized.
But then again, maybe it isn't.

Maybe there is still a light in the dark.

Pretentious Poem III

A dim light,
a faint glimmer
of hope

that I hold onto
for dear life.

Proof positive
but inconclusive—

maybe, maybe not.

But it's all
I got. So

I still hold on,
until you let go.
And even then

I won't say no.
I'll never say no.

Rapture?

I await
your return,
like a Christian
awaits
The Second Coming
of Christ.

I—
having something
in common
with the Christian
(for a change)—

absolutely no
guarantee
whatsoever
that either Christ
or you
will show up
anytime soon,
if ever.

The difference
is that
I can admit it,

whereas the Christian,
where Christ's coming

is concerned,
will most likely deny it.

However,
both the Christian
and I
act purely
on faith.

But at this point,

it seems that
the Christian
has the advantage
over me,

for I think that
Christ
has one up on you.

Yes—

I want the inside track.
Yes— I want to pull
away from the pack.

Bottom line:
I want you
as a part of
my life,

even if it's
only a fraction
of the whole.

Yes.

A chance

to touch you
deep—

bind us
together,

permanently.

Take it.

Get sticky.

Endgame

All right.
This is it.

Things are not good
(or they could be great).

You are now
outside of the
Borderline,
confirmed.

This is ten seconds
left in the fourth quarter
with one play left.
Damn it.

Once again,
the ball is in the air.
But this time,
it's definitely gonna come down,
soon. Very soon.

And I feel
that you are triple covered.
You might make the effort, but—
you could be overpowered.
Bottom line—

this ends here.
Or it begins again.

If it ends, then
what of it?
No, seriously.

It's like taking a path
that leads to nowhere,
then turning around and

taking the other path
that comes out exactly
where the first ended up—
nowhere.

But if it begins again,
it would begin again
afresh, anew,
with no Border restrictions.

I would like that.
Would you? Yes,
possibly but—

it could also bring about
a new set of restrictions—
actually, not new, but now
more realized.

I, for one, would like
that kind of salvation,
even if it meant that I

would now be in bondage
to a new slave master. But hey,
that's salvation: a new type
of slavery.

At least, we would be
bound together.

But like it was with her,
it's up to you.

It's entirely up to you.

Or maybe not entirely.

...incomplete.

I hate good-byes.
There's been far too many
of them lately,
and I just can't accept
the fact—
with her, with you,
with others.

Editorial comment:
there's something very
fucked up
with this aspect of life.

"It's a dream." Well, then—
wake me up, already.
Wake us all up
while you're at it, for

I've been asleep.
We've *all* been asleep
too God damned long.

Circumstances
situations
that keep us apart

forces
beyond our
control

the ol'
Second Law
of Thermodynamics
once again

and that day—
did I accelerate
our entropy?
I wonder.

Someday

Girl—
if you must
go away,
go away.

But
if you can
stay

and get in touch,
get in touch.

Reach out
and touch me—

a standing offer.

Good bye.

That's all.

I have nothing left to say.

I have nothing left—

I have nothing—

I have—

I.

PROJECTIONS

(Bet. 4/22-30/05)

"To make a start,
out of particulars
and make them general, rolling
up the sum, by defective means—"

(From "Paterson"— William Carlos Williams)

In a dream
we met

one last
time

one night
at a

country
kiosk

in the middle
of nowhere

but nowhere
seems beautiful

and you're
there

similarly
beautiful

behind the
register

intoxicated
out of control

not from drink
from situations

beyond your
control

you flirt
and lean in close

giving me
a long passionate kiss

that tastes
sweet

but then
you leave

the transaction
incomplete

A pretty
girl

takes your
place

whom you and I
both know

a mutual
friend

a help to us
in the past

but it didn't
last

she has no
control

over the
situation so

the transaction
remains

incomplete
She leaves

and I am left
standing there

alone there
tempted to

complete it myself
but I don't dare

bring myself
to it

I also
lack control So

the transaction
remains

incomplete
And incomplete

it stays as
I stand

there alone
until closing

until night
alone

and walk
away

down a
tree lined

driveway
and through

the iron
gate

Shiny black
pants

and platforms
under

a full
moon

of possibility
as we

await

the second
coming